TWO B

Poems by John Cotton and Fred Sedgwick

James Daniel Daniel John Press

Second edition James Daniel Daniel John Press 1996
85 Cliff Lane
Ipswich
Suffolk
First Published by Mary Glasgow Publications, 1990

Illustrations by Sarah Fisher, Daniel Sedgwick and children from Peartree Spring Infant and St Nicholas Primary Schools, Stevenage
Cover illustration by MESH
Printed by The Ipswich Book Company Ltd., Suffolk
ISBN 0 9523185 39

For Tamsin and Daniel

CONTENTS

Tomorrow I'm going to the fair

Tomorrow I'm going to the fair.
The others in our class'll be there,
coins stuffed into anoraks,
crashing round the dodgem tracks.

Tomorrow I'm going to the fair.
Jessica Jackson-Wood'll be there
on the Flying Rolletto as high as high
while her mother squints at the terrible sky.

The boys from Inkerman Street will be in
the Ghost Train making a ghostly din.
They'll suck at candy floss, and smoke,
and go home loud and happy and broke.

Tomorrow I'm going to the fair.
There's nothing on earth that can compare
with the raucous light, and the flashing sound
as Jessie and I whirl the dodgems around. **F.S.**

Norman and Margaret Watkins

Norman and Margaret Watkins
    lived on a river boat.
He owned an electrical guitar
    but couldn't sing a note.

Margaret's voice was sweet as Sunday
    when raindrops pour and pour;
exciting as your Grandad Duncan
    talking about the war.

Norman and Margaret sang and sang
    and sang to the willow trees
and the willow trees sang back to them
    "Stop it, the pair of you, please!"

Norman and Margaret lived a life
    exactly where it was at
while the river wished they'd live their life
    in a twenty-fourth storey flat.

They sang early one morning
    of a girl and her gipsy kin...
and the river rose in a tidal fury
    and hauled the pair of them in.

Norman and Margaret Watkins'
    screams sounded just the same
as the songs they'd tortured the river with -
    only a little more tame.

Norman and Margaret Watkins
    died, and the river roared
a Hallelujah Chorus
    with a deafening unison chord.   **F.S.**

A pirate

There once was a pirate called Pete
Who would dance on one leg for a treat.
Well the other was wooden
So it's quite understooden
That he frequently fell on his seat! **J.C.**

Camping

Once a year we would go to camp,
Humping our kitbags to where
The lorry would take them off to Devon.
Then by train and coach we sped away from town
To a field where the moors rolled away like the sea,
The woods were as dark as caves
And the spring water tasted sharp as a knife.
We heaved the heavy canvas of bell tents up on their poles,
To which our feet would point at night
As we lay in our blankets like spokes in a wheel.
And the youngest of us would wake long before the others,
Lying still and watching, through the triangle of doorway,
The shifting light of dawn, the mist dispersing,
And listening to the mysterious dry-throated call of the distant
wood pigeons.
We felt alone and strangers in a world
Where the true citizens were the ponies and sheep
In the fields close by,
Yet sensing, for all that,
That we had returned to what was ours. **J.C.**

Morning song

The world takes shape
under my hand.
Light develops
a slow movie
of these swans on
the first river,
this first wind-swayed
tree. Birdsong begins.
The evening and
the morning are
the sixth day. I
lift my hand and
compose my first
Sunday morning hymn.
From that hazel
copse a man and
a woman walk. **F.S.**

Only

Only a tap drip, dripping
In the courtyard, by the wall
Where cushiony mosses flourish
And fleshy ferns grow tall.
Only a shutter rattling
When the wind decides to call,
Only a creeping of shadows
As night begins to fall.
Only a whisper of memories
In the lonely air of the hall. **J.C.**

Skipping rhyme

Over the 'in'
over the 'out',
Arthur McDonnelly's
up the spout.

The battlements on
the castle wall
are sure to crumble
and to fall.

The cracks they shot
the arrows through
are blocked to Arthur
McDonnelly's view.

Down in the dungeon,
prisoners gone,
there's only a broken up
skeleton.

A scuffling noise?
Only a rat
twenty feet down -
no fear of that.

Over the 'in',
over the 'out',
Arthur McDonnelly's
up the spout.

He'll lie tonight
all sleek and fat
under the drip
of the cider vat.

He'll never kill
a man again
till something whispers
to Arthur 'When'.

Over the 'in',
over the 'out',
Arthur McDonnelly's
up the spout. **F.S.**

Playtime rhyme

Salt and kitchen, rain and mustard -
put your head into this custard.
When it starts to be a pain
salt and kitchen, mustard, rain.

Salt, mustard, rain and kitchen -
round the table kids and pitch in.
When you've had enough, get down.
Some ginger beer, and off to town.

Mustard. Kitchen. Rain. Salt.
It isn't mine, it's all your fault.
I'm telling them that it was you.
I don't care what you will do.

Salt and kitchen, mustard, rain -
watch my hopes go down the drain.
Indoor play, let's shout and sing,
and muck about like anything. **F.S.**

The gourmets

The Rovers have won, it is Saturday night
And Ginger and me are feeling quite bright.
We're both growing lads so we need lots of nosh
So we go in for quantity rather than posh.
So after our tea of eggs and boiled ham,
Fried bread and toast with lashing of jam,
It's off to the Pie Shop for Joe's mushy peas
Which we help to wash down with several teas.
Then it's round to the 'Indian' for a quick vindaloo
With chappaties and dhall with Mr Chindoo.
We drop into the pub to wish our friends cheers
And take in pork scratchings and a couple of beers.
Time now for the 'Chinese' with bean shoots and spring rolls
Which we eat with soy sauce from dragony bowls.
At the Doner-Kebab, in a van round the corner,
We eat skewers of meat which makes us feel warmer
Both inside and out, but we have to be nippy
To get to 'Aunt May's' before she closes the Chippy!
There some cod and a bagful of chips sets us up
Before stopping at Sam's for a wedge and a cup
Of hot cocoa at his all-night under-arch stall.
"Any more?" asks Sam. "Thanks, that just about all",
We say as we go home, feeling all right
Having eaten our way through Saturday night. **J.C.**

Snow

Snow is a blanket
Silently pulled over the town at night,
Softening both sound and shapes so all in sight
Is quietly muffled, smooth and bland.
Shapes lose their character and all the land
Is levelled as if neatly wrapped
Like a great white parcel
And all mapped
Landmarks are lost.

The scratchy holly's
Now a soft-skinned ball,
And mounds and shrubs and plants have all
Disappeared, while a cold lid has closed
Over the pond's bright eye.
We marvel at it. Then from the sky
The sun's slow burn
Will see the world we know
Gradually return. **J.C.**

A garden's seasons

Spring:
A bud bursting
Grass growing
Nest building
May white
Day bright
Between showery season.

Summer:
A flower unfolding
Sun golding
Bee buzzing
Heat-haze fuzzing
Colour courting
Hope of a season.

Autumn:
A rusty, scarlet
Leaf littering
Seed swelling
Misty hazing
Frost crazing
Berry burgeoning season.

Winter:
A short-dayed
Icicle fringed
Christmas binged
Snow whiting
Bone biting
Rough old dog of a season. **J.C.**

The best bed

The best bed's a single bed,
the best bed of all.
There's football posters all around
the bedroom wall.

There's piles and piles of Asterix books
and comics everywhere
and if you say the room's a mess
I don't care.

The best bed's a trampoline
and the best bed's a ship
where the sea's a carpet strewn with things,
a proper tip.

The best bed's where my mother comes
and kisses me, and all
the football players are smiling down
from my wall. **F.S.**

Syllabics (our class)

Rachael 7 plays cello
and does immaculate sums.
She writes about her yellow
goldfish and her twin brothers
as if they're all worth the same!
Cellist, peace-maker, poet,
She will inherit the earth.

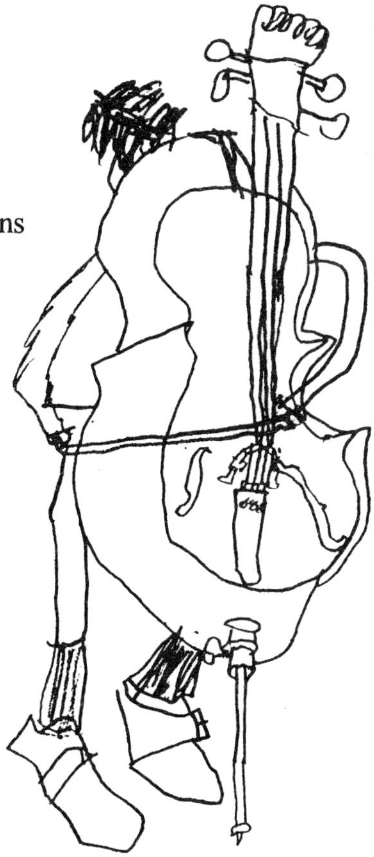

Sylvia 6 is a
terrible creature, a
girl who can frighten the
strictest of teachers. She
call them bad names and runs
out of the gate, and she -

Elena 5 has
five digits of course
on each dirty hand;
five thoughts in her head:
castles in the sand.

Anna 4 calls
for me each day.
We walk to school
past waterfalls.

Ida 3
carved our names
on the tree.

Jo 2
loves you! **F.S.**

A day out in the car

The sun's out, the sky clear,
Let's go out in the car,
We could drive to the seaside
It's not all that far.

There's Brighton or Hove,
Or Goring-on-Sea,
We could get there by
lunch time
And stay until tea.

We packed a quick picnic
Of salad and cake,
With apples and Tizer
For a mid-morning break.

So it was we set out
Passing Redhill and Horley,
The Airport at Gatwick
And then on to Crawley.

We sped on to Horsham,
Southwater and Rock,
It was there we first saw
The Downs and a flock

Of fleecy white sheep
Grazing on the green slopes,
And sensed the first scent
Of the sea and our hopes.

At Worthing we put on
Our costumes to swim,
While Grandmother paddled
And old Uncle Jim

Flopped out in a deck chair
To soak in the sun,
While Dad read the paper
To see what had won

In the races at Brighton.
Then after our dip
We tucked into lunch
And started to flip

Some water at Mum,
Who got a bit cross
So we thought we'd best leave it
And instead went across

To buy some ice cream
From a hut by the shore.
After sandcastles and cricket,
Though we would have
liked more,

The shadows got longer
And we all grew to know
That our time had run out
And it was time to go.

As we sped along roads
On our way back to Ealing
The reddening sunset
And the dusk left us feeling

Drowsily cheerful
As we dozed in the deep
Seats of the car,
And soon were asleep,

Happily dreaming
Of a splendid day past,
And while it had gone
The memories would last. **J.C.**

Mementoes

There's a place
in our garden
where the lawn's worn bare
by my goalie dives

and under the settee
in the front room
there's a pile
of Dick King-Smith books

that are falling apart.
In the bathroom
there's talc
in a bear-shaped bottle;

and the kitchen cupboards
are filled with things
my parents never eat or
drink:
Appletize, tomato ketchup,

Cocopops, chocolate spread.
My drawings improve
the walls of our house
everywhere:

my monsters, my elephant,
my pyramids. Photos
abound, too
where my parents work.

Me on my second birthday,
me in the temple at Karnak,
making a face. Or running
after Oscar the dog...

When I sleep round Joe's
my parents look
at these things
and wish I was home

so I could ruin the lawn.
They look in my bedroom
in the morning
and say "Shall I get him
now?"

Then I am a prince
welcomed back to the
kingdom.
I untidy things again
and de-silence the rooms.

F.S.

Face lift

The thatcher plays ladders
On the roof, and trusts
There are no snakes
In his particular game
As he pins and layers
The new blonde wig,
And the brickie repoints
Those ageing wrinkles
On the brow.
The glazier whitens the
bright
New contact lenses
So she will not glimpse
Reflections
Before the eye-liners
Of lintel and sill
Are touched in.
A new door firms-up
Mouth and chin.
While the plumber
Encases the varicose pipes,
And the plasterer
Strokes the wall's skin
To a bland smoothness.
In the yard
The cement mixer's
Digestion worsens
As it retches
Stones and sand,
And the lime pit
Burns and glowers
At the clouds hovering
In its watery eye.

J.C.

Cleaning windows

They're cleaning windows
in the classroom:
a man worships
the buddleia's roots
as he drags his black line
across the glass.
His friend focuses
on the blankness
in front of him.

In the time it takes
to think of going home
Joey, the friendly one, sweeps
an archipelago of stains
to nothing
and smiles at me.

The quiet one feels
the backs of his knees
then stands, flexes each leg
and turns his attention
to the high window
over the cupboard
where they store the huge maps
of England and Wales,
The British Isles,
Europe, the Northern Hemisphere
the World, the Solar System...

Up there I can see
a tired man at work
on a perfect
rectangle of sky. **F.S.**

The leg of a pig

A man visiting a farm pointed out one of the pigs as a remarkable animal. "Indeed," said the farmer, "that pig is remarkable. When our son fell into the pond that pig dived in and saved his life. Later, when the farmhouse caught fire, that pig telephoned the Fire Brigade and saved all our lives."

"Why has it got only three legs?" the visitor asked.

"When you've got a pig as remarkable as that, you don't eat it all at once."

Old joke

They gave it to Dolly
Because she was jolly -

The leg of a pig
The leg of a pig.

They gave it to Louisa
Because it would please her -

The leg of a pig,
The leg of a pig.

They gave it to Berty
Because he was flirty -

The leg of a pig,
The leg of a pig.

They gave it to Peggy
Because she was leggy -

The leg of a pig,
The leg of a pig.

They gave it to Alice
To take to the Palace -

The leg of a pig,
The leg of a pig.

They gave it to Prunella
To give to a fella -

The leg of a pig,
The leg of a pig.

They gave it to Mary
Although she was wary -

The leg of a pig,
The leg of a pig.

They gave it to Clare
Because she would share -

The leg of a pig,
The leg of a pig.

They gave it to Jerry
Because he was merry -

The leg of a pig,
The leg of a pig.

They gave it to Oscar
For singing his Tosca -

The leg of a pig,
The leg of a pig.

They gave it to Dawn
Whose knickers were torn -

The leg of a pig,
The leg of a pig.

They gave it to Faye
Who gave it away -

The leg of a pig,
The leg of a pig. **J.C.**

Through that door

Through that door
Is a garden with a wall,
The red brick crumbling,
The lupins growing tall,
Where the lawn is like a carpet
Spread for you,
And it's all as tranquil
As you never knew.

Through that door
Is the great ocean-sea
Which heaves and rolls
To eternity,
With its islands and promontories
Waiting for you
To explore and discover
In that vastness of blue.

Through that door
Is your secret room
Where the window lets in
The light of the moon,
With its mysteries and magic
Where you can find
Thrills and excitements
Of every kind.

Through that door
Are the mountains and the moors
And the rivers and the forests
Of the great outdoors,
All the plains and the ice-caps
And lakes as blue as sky
For all those creatures
That walk or swim or fly.

Through that door
Is the city of the mind
Where you can imagine
What you'll find.
You can make of that city
What you want it to,
And if you choose to share it,
Then it could come true. **J.C.**

Listen

Silence is when you can hear things.
Listen:
The breathing of bees,
A moth's foot fall,
Or the mist easing its way
Across the field,
The light shifting at dawn
Or the stars clicking into place
At evening. **J.C.**

Night

The full moon's bowl
Pours out its liquid light.
All colour gone
The scene is starkly bright,
Deep wells of darkness,
Shallow pools of light.
While from an upstairs window
A frost bleached field
Is a lake that floods
Far out into the weald.
The road's river glistens
On which the vehicles ride,
And flaky moths
Are bobbing on the tide
Of air. The white-rigged owl,
Which drifts from barn to tree,
Ghost-ships it on the airy sea.
Meanwhile the wary mouse
Finds its safe harbour
In a nearby house.
The world is theirs
During these moonlit hours,
Until the dawn breaks
And once more it's ours. **J.C.**

Exploring the rock pool

We explore the rock pool,
A small world of its own:
The scuttling crab, quick shrimps,
Sea-polished stone
With hints of colours
Enhanced by the light-
Refracting water
Making all so bright.
The strands of seaweed
Verdant, sleek as silk,
The tiny limpets
Shells white as milk.
A sea in miniature
Which lasts just for a day,
When the tide renews it
Washing the old away. **J.C.**

Turn your back behind you

"Turn your back behind you, and say no more to me,
For if you do I'll cut your throat, and tie you to a tree."

- heard at Chardstock in Devon,
by Iona and Peter Opie

Turn your back behind you,
stay away from me.
I no longer want you
to climb the apple tree.
I no longer want to
whisper tales with you
or dig into the sycamore,
John ♥ Helen TRUE.

Turn your back behind you,
leave me with my ball
to throw against the blank part
of the ivy wall.
Soon James will come, and Marion,
eyes and voices free -
so turn your back behind you
and stay away from me.

Turn your back behind you,
step through the garden gate.
If you come here again, come here
never, or very late.
Go from this room's window
as fast as you will
and laugh with James and Marion
on the summer hill.

The apple tree is waiting,
the sycamore stands still
and crawls with life and wind among
my mother's daffodils.
Oh, turn your back behind you.
Leave me while I wait
for James and Marion to run
by my garden gate. **F.S.**

Old Mr de la Mare

Old Mr de la Mare
Sits in the sun
And the poems come and chatter
And chatter and come.

De la Mare, sometimes,
Reads to me
And I listen and pine
For my dear t.v.

Old Mr de la Mare
And Nicholas Nye
And Goodie McTavish
All stroll by.

Old Sally Worm
And Mrs McQueen,
Old Tillie Turveycombe
Can still be seen.

They all come strolling
And my Uncle Walter
Reads on and on and on
And he doesn't falter.

Old Mr de la Mare
Sits in the shade
And I think about my telly
And my lemonade. **F.S.**

Fruit and veg

Cherry

We are the cherry family,
All cheerful on our plate,
And later, if you count our stones,
We could tell you your fate.

Banana

Canary coloured and shaped like a boat,
It's my soft sweet taste that gets your vote.
But when at last you've eaten me all,
Beware my skin which can make you fall!

Orange

I am a bright round orange,
Quite sun-like in my beauty,
Peel off my skin and then you'll find
Me succulent and fruity.

Plum

A plum, my skin's so deep, deep blue
Like a night without a moon.
With cousin apple I make fine pies,
Et mon grandpere est une prune.

Pineapple

My face may be rough and quite scaly,
And my hair is a bit like a punk's;
But inside I'm sweet and a bit of a treat
With ice cream and cut up in chunks.

Radish

I am a raw red radish
All sharp and fresh and munchy,
My skin is red, my flesh is white
And hot and crisp and crunchy. **J.C.**

What the headteacher said when he saw me running out of school at 1.15 pm. on 21 July last year to buy an ice cream from Pellozzi's van

Hey!*

F.S.

*This poem is an attempt on three world records at once: the longest title, the longest footnote, and the shortest text of any poem in the western world. It has been lodged with *The Guinness Book of Records*.

Torches

It is the torches I remember best.
Going home on a winter's evening
We would point them skyward,
Screwing the fronts to sharpen the pencils of light
That they might pierce the darkness the better.
Bold young challengers of stars
We competed in length and brightness.
Yes, better than the chips,
Tart with vinegar and salt grains,
In bags like small grease-proof hats,
Better even than the large orange bottles,
Tizer tasting of fruit that never was,
Were the torches,
Their beams like friendly knives
Making cuts in a darkness
Which oh so quickly healed
At the touch of a switch. **J.C.**

Michael MacIntosh and I

As I stepped into sunlight this morning
I thought the whole thing through:
You'll be kind as cake to me
And I'll be kind to you.

Yesterday, in the rainstorm
Under the Nelson Oak
We clashed like admirals because
I couldn't take a joke.

Now sun laughs from behind the hill
And brightens Hardy Ground.
Wagtails trot, and sparrows quarrel
And starlings stab around.

Today things will be fine, and battles
Are skirmishes in the past.
Michael MacIntosh and I
Are partners that will last...

But the brilliant sun was just too bright.
Leaves scratched at my face.
Crossly I started to run, and Michael
Easily won the race.

Now I sit in the classroom this morning
Putting sums in a perfect row
Feeling his world avoiding mine,
Like a gigantic no.

Oh Michael under the Nelson Oak
Picking a team for a game,
I'll laugh like the sun at your silly joke
If you'll only call my name. **F.S.**

Long distance information

(for Dawn and Daniel)

'My uncle took the message
And he wrote it on the wall'
Chuck Berry

At the crossroads by Mr Lee's teashop
  Where Daniel once fell from his bike
A man and a woman are jiving and singing
  A song that Dan and I like.

It's about a bridge and a sunset.
  We listen with eyes and ears wide
To the airman who sings his American song
  With his beautiful Suffolker bride.

I imagine the broad Mississippi
  Bridge, and a man saying Hi
To Marie, his daughter a hundred-odd miles
  Off. And he starts to cry.

But this couple are laughing and dancing
  To the tune they have chosen today
And Dan and I sit here and listen
  Till the spell fades, and we drive away. **F.S.**

Horse chestnuts

Autumn's special toys,
There is something about the newness of them,
Their gloss, the colour of burnished horses,
Their richness protected from their fall
By those thick green cases,
So that we can harvest them
Safe in their nests
Of last year's debris of leaves,
To pocket them
For treasures or for play.
Though they will never be
Quite so beautiful again,
As that first moment
When we saw them peep pristine
From their soft-spiked shells. **J.C.**

Moorland signals

Behind the stone cottage
the wife pegs out her washing,
a bright bunting
of challenge to the grey
power of the moor
which, like the vasts
of a terrestrial sea, casts
up, from time to time,
a pony or a sheep.
Out of the mists and rime
such visitors stare at night
at the homing beacon
of the cottage's square of light. **J.C.**

A life

Born on a Monday
And hung out to dry.
Hungry on Tuesday
So we give out a cry.
When we reach Wednesday
We set out for school,
Showing by Thursday
We're nobody's fool.
Freedom by Friday
We're growing up fast.
Shouting by Saturday
That sadness is past.
So serenely on Sunday
We build dreams that won't last. **J.C.**

The film

Clearing the house we found
Your old box camera,
Put away long before
You left for hospital,
And in it an exposed film.
A red roll on a black spool,
What would the Chemist's
Wake from this chrysalis
Of time?

It unrolled to a back garden,
A son and daughter's visit,
A grandchild skipping on the grass,
And you sitting, content, in the last
Sunshine of your last summer.
So close, so intimate,
So special as to be
Without point to others, yet
In its very ordinariness
Saying everything. **J.C.**

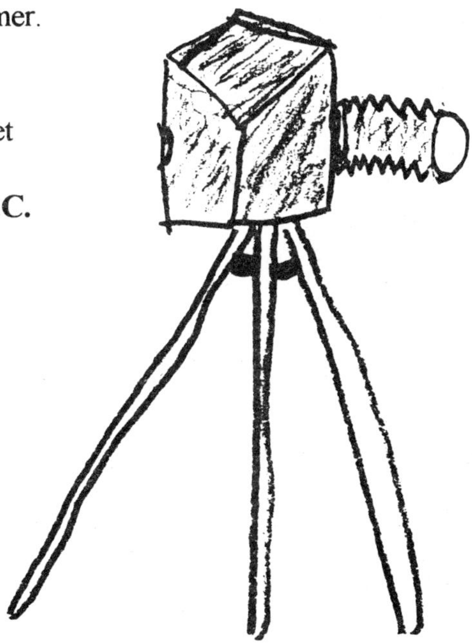

Two gardens

Deaf Eric's garden's bright with flowers.
    Mine's a shambles.
He kneels and hoes in his, all hours.
Mine's sycamore seedlings, bindweed, brambles,
knobbly grass that cripples mowers,
shrubs where a broken deckchair cowers.

Deaf Eric grows: sprouts, cabbages, runner beans, lettuces and
    kholrabi.

I grow: babies, metal rods, spent fireworks, newspapers and
    elderly gentlemen.

Deaf Eric stands in hearing aid
    and patched jacket.
He looks around at the joy he's made,
sees a weed, and bends to hack it,
tiptoes across the lawn he laid
and sips a glass of lemonade.

I pick up: Jodie from next door, a car aerial, a Roman Candle, last
    Sunday's Observer supplement and Mr Burns Elliot from the
    Post Office.

Deaf Eric shakes a silent head
    across the road.
Recalls when cops gave up for dead
a Jehovah's Witness, Mr Joad
who'd said "Your garden's charming, Fred..."
and walked in, minus fear or dread...

He'd survived a year in my garden shed
on conference pears and berries red
and bacon rind and crumbs of bread...

Deaf Eric's garden's bright with flowers.
Mine's a shambles...   **F.S.**

Fireworks

First there was the eager looking forward
As hoarded in the safety of biscuit tins
Those bright cardboard buds awaited their flowering.
When, at a match's touch came
The sudden and immediate joy of crackle and colour
And the rocket's fiery upward rush.
Then last, the early morning's pleasure
(The night's smoke still on the air)
Of searching for the spent cases,
The charred and burnt out husks,
The scorched rocket dew-drenched on its stick,
Something that might actually have soared
As high as our hopes. **J.C.**

Things they say

Grow up girl.
Tidy your room.
Don't shuffle under the table.
Put the cat down
and don't kick the dog.
Don't give me that stuff, it's a fable.

Don't eat that plum.
Where are your manners?
Go, now, and see Mrs Brown.
Get down the shops
and buy me some tights
and don't hang around in the town.

I've told you before
and how many times
must I tell you to empty that bin?
Don't open that door
and don't close that window...
Just wait till your father gets in.

Grow up girl.
Tidy your room
or you won't see that game on t.v.
If those things aren't away
when I come up again
you'll have to answer to me. **F.S.**

Good morning, boys and girls

Today I would like to show you
the surest way to win
a few bob on the horses
but as I've never left
a racecourse with my shirt
I'd better start assembly
in a more customary way:
So let's sing our first hymn
'Roll out the barrel'...

Now boys and girls there's something
my mother used to tell me
and I'm going to tell it to you.
It doesn't matter what you do,
as long as (now listen carefully)
nobody catches you at it.

Let's list some dreadful things:
hiding your grandfather's glasses,
terrifying the parrots
in the exotic bird enclosure
at Colchester Zoo, and hoping
they'll squawk and swear; spreading
alarm in the Old People's Home
with rumours about wars...
writing words on the toilet wall...

The trick is, don't get caught.
Learn the subtle rhythms
of your parents' and teachers' tread;
be able to recognise
all official uniforms:
police officer, obviously,
referee, zoo attendant,
nurse and traffic warden
and, quite possibly, soldier,
at a glance from a hundred yards...
and if you're finally caught
lie your way out of it.

When in doubt, then, think of my mother
and what she said to me...

Now about today:
Do what you please;
run on the roof screaming the name
of your football team;
play space-games on the computer;
disco-dance all morning
in the hall till you're flat out,
and them come to me or Ms Mayers
for your Exports and Special Brews
or (and I mean the infants, here, really)
your shandy or ginger beer.
If you feel like a read
there's piles of Tintin books
and comics outside my door...

Now before we sing our last hymn
are there any notices?
The cheating at tests club will meet
at twelve in the music room...
Thank you Ms Mayers. And there's
hacking practice on the field at one -
- thank you, Mr Simmonds. Anything else? Oh yes...
could you let me have your orders for lunch time drinks
at least by morning play.
And I'm sorry, boys and girls,
but I can only supply
additive-enriched crisps...

Now, our final hymn
is one of my favourites.
Let's sing it with great feeling:
Let's sing it for the last time -
Mr Suit and Mrs Pearl
and several of their friends
are gathering at the back,
ready to take me away.
A chord, please, Ms Mayers.
All together now,
'Show me the way to go home...

All right, all right, Mr Suit,
I'm coming quietly...
Goodbye boys and girls... **F.S.**

Christmas day in the suburbs

How hushed the day is,
No one is around,
The streets are empty
There is hardly a sound.
The frost has touched the garden
With purifying white,
Even the birds are silent
And keeping out of sight. **J.C.**

A snowing globe

Inside the glass globe it will snow to order.
A shake and the storm begins,
And while the whiteness swirls about them
The top-hatted gentleman and the full-skirted lady
Are as unmoving as their small brightly painted house
And the wooden trees beside it.
Soon all is still, the tranquil scene restored.
We look in at this miniature enclosed world,
Safe in its predictability,
And give it another shake,
Secure in knowing the storm cannot harm it. **J.C.**

In the kitchen

In the kitchen
After the aimless
Chatter of the plates,
The murmurings of the gas,
The chuckle of the water pipes
And the sharp exchanges
Of knives, forks and spoons,
Comes the serious quiet,
When the sink slowly clears its throat
And you can hear the occasional rumble
Of the refrigerator's tummy
As it digests the cold. **J.C.**

Seven riddles

1.

I am one of an endless
family,
My brothers and sisters
Never far behind.
I crash and swirl,
Grind pebbles, growl,
And gnaw the bones of the
land
Like a great wet dog.

J.C.

2.

My momentary delights
Are held close
In a paper bud,
I flower best at night,
My petals falling
Like bright showers
When I am fired to beauty.

J.C.

3.

I am a see-through pear
Hanging from my treeless branch.
A bit of a conjuror, I can ripen suddenly,
Or disappear at the touch of a switch.
Like the apple I am good for you
Lengthening your days. **J.C.**

4.

I am at your beginning and your end.
I dog your footsteps
And cannot be shaken off.
Though I fade from view
You are never alone.
So silent that you often forget me,
I am still there,
Your constant dark spy and companion. **J.C.**

5.

Within white seamless walls
I store my treasure,
A gold that nourishes.
Search as you will
You will find no opening in me.
Once shattered I am not for mending. **J.C.**

6. The Biggest Riddle

I take you with me
As you watch me passing by.
A traveller, I am constantly
Crossing a frontier
From which there is no return.
Always present
You are only sure of me when I'm gone.
You try to measure me,
But I am measureless in the end,
Being without end.
I am that abstraction
In which you live. **J.C.**

7. An Even Bigger Riddle

You take a pew
to study my worth
while others adore
their cars in the Sabbath sun.

I have so many names,
so many natures
and quarrelling about them,
you cross me time and time again.

I am not small black books in a row.
I am the silent word
walking in the garden
in the cool of day. **F.S.**

The answers to these 7 riddles are on page 53

In the woods

In the woods we would quietly skirt
That area where we could just glimpse,
Through the brambles,
A makeshift shelter of tarpaulin and sticks,
And, occasionally, movement or a drift of smoke.
We never went nearer,
Nor thought of doing so.
It wasn't fear so much,
Though that was part of it,
But the sense of a secret, alien life
Which we furnished with our imagination,
And was worth keeping a mystery. **J.C.**

Fog

He creeps in stealthily at morning or at night,
Soft-footed, masked, a thief -
Come to steal our light,
So that the houses loom shapeless and grey,
Trees are smudges and we lose our way.
When even our lights look pale and dim,
For he'd steal those too if it was left to him!
Damp and murky he will make you cough
Until our friend the sun sees him off.
When it will be as if he'd never been
And nothing of him anywhere can be seen.
So we forget him, until one night
He sneaks in again to give us a fright. **J.C.**

John Crystal

John Crystal was the kindest teacher
    I ever had:
More generous than rain on grass
    But many times as sad.

For Johnny Crystal, he could not
    Control his fountain pen
Let alone the boys then changing
    Into gentlemen.

There were a hundred ways that we
    Eclipsed John Crystal's sun:
"What did you do in school today?"
    "We had a bit of fun..."

Then one Monday night I walked
    Back for something I'd
Forgotten in the mayhem of
    Skinning Crystal's hide.

Past the headmaster's office and
    Through empty rooms I move.
They're quiet as the time before
    Needle touches groove.

Then, *piano*, comes the sound
    Of the gentlest kind of jazz
From one of the treasured records that,
    I'm sure, my father has.

I nudge the hall door open.
    His gown slung on a chair,
His head a-sway to silent drums,
    John Crystal's playing there.

His eyes are closed, his tie is loose.
    On the piano stand
His coffee mug and ashtray
    At the beck of his hand.

Now, John Crystal, when I hear
    Brubeck and Desmond play
I think of how we tortured you
    Day after cruel day.

I think of all the times the sun
    Went dim across your world
Because of the gentlemanly wit
    We nobly hurled.

I see your full head swaying
    And your discarded gown
And hear the fractured melody
    Even I couldn't drown. **F.S.**

Winter song

"I've been here too long"
Says the Man in the Moon,
Floating over the tops
Of the hazels in Hazel Copse.
    "I've sung my song".

"Same goes for me too"
Says Jack Frost, crisply.
"Want to be on my own
For a good think, a moan.
    My sparkling is through".

It's all gone too far.
Santa's waited and sweated
In his last grotto
With his last doll and Lotto,
    Transformer and car.

And Winter and Frost
And the Moon turn in
On themselves. Girls and boys
Search out a new noise
    For the ones lost.

"What's that?" say the lakes
As the new words swirl
Over stone ground
    Like leaves.

        "It's the sound
    The children's song makes".   **F.S.**

Writing about the rain

The first thing was
we got wet

but we didn't mind.
Our parents grumbled

and our cars clogged the roads
but we enjoyed the puddles

and the wet-leaved branches
that swung and scattered

another, rougher christening
in our faces.

And the next thing
was shouting, pulling,

pushing boots off
in the cloakroom;

hanging things on hooks,
leaving little lakes on the floor;

and the last thing was
them saying

Look at the rain
darkening the world you know.

You're Adam, you're Eve.
See it for the first time...

and we wrote this. **F.S.**

Four minutes

There'd been a fight
    down our street
Sunday: two men,
    both older than my Dad -

and sometimes today
    at this desk
I can't concentrate
    on Kes or Mockingbird

for the sight
    in my mind's eye
of that powerful
    curly-haired man

his small minder
    was leading away,
tender persuasive
    fingers reaching

to a burning cheek.
    They didn't glance
uphill or down
    for Sunday traffic.

He was so angry,
    his minder was so bald.
None of us could stop
            looking
    till they were two men
        from Lowry.

The fury and compassion
    shrank as their backs
            went
down the next street.
    I think I will

remember the day
    the world's beginning
to end that angry man
    and his bald, kind minder,

those fingers, that livid
            cheek,
    how the men became
in four minutes
    the human race

and disappeared.   **F.S.**

Three adults at school

Ms Ann Potter, secretary

types the letters. and is very
loving when you cut your knee
(she's a mother, too, you see).
She murmurs "Poor old Melanie!
the ground got in your way again?..."
She cleans it, dries it - "there!" - and then
sends you laughing on your way.
Other jobs she does all day
are: calculating, making tea,
looking after Ms King: she
wouldn't be fit to boss at all
without Ms Potter at her call.
She doesn't flap when angry parents
noisily make their appearance
shouting "I'll have that Mrs Brown!
I'll drag her by the hair through town,
I will, I'll -" "Mr Rowson-Hoffey,
would you like a cup of coffee?
Sugar? Two? And milk? Of course..."
Mr Rowson-Hoffey, hoarse
from shouting, meakly whispers, "Please..."
and holds his cup upon his knees.
She keeps inspectors at the gate
by singing hymn one-fifty-eight
from Childhood Praise. The teachers rate
her number one, and they don't know
half the skills she has to show.
At night, at home, she sees her John
to bed, and puts a record on:
Mozart, Bach, or Richard Strauss
obediently fills the house.
Her mind at last is calm, as she
pours another cup of tea. **F.S.**

Name change

Mrs Clayton
classroom helper
used to be Miss Pratt
swopped rings quickly at the altar
murmured
Oh
my goodness gracious!
Thank the Lord for that!

Oh my goodness gracious
thank the Lord for that. **F.S.**

A limerick

A nursery teacher, Ms Price
was frightened of gerbils and mice
and hamsters and rats
and rabbits and cats...
but she rode on a Bactrian, twice. **F.S.**

Going to bed

Daniel, time for bed now -
Look, you're on your knees!
Pale and cross and desperate
for your pillow. Please!

It's long past your bedtime
and tomorrow you've
got school to go to. Come
on,
come on Daniel, move!

Your mum and I are tired,
drained as dogs and would
like to hit the sack quite
soon
if we only could.

OK Mummy, Daddy -
you can go to bed
and I will bring some cocoa
up
and tuck you up instead.

Make sure behind your ears
is
clean as it should be,
I'll just sit up another hour
or two or maybe three.

I'll tell you some stories
of treason on the seas -
so up you go, my darling
parents -

Daniel! Bedtime! Please!

F.S.

Answers to the *Seven riddles*

1. Wave 2. Firework 3. Light bulb
4. Shadow 5. Egg 6. Time 7. God